What do you call an u[...]
Great Dane?

Scooby-Dude.

Terror-rific Joke Book

501 029 391

PUFFIN BOOKS

Published by the Penguin Group
Penguin Books Ltd, 80 Strand, London WC2R 0RL, England
Penguin Group (USA) Inc., 375 Hudson Street, New York, New York 10014, USA
Penguin Group (Canada), 10 Alcorn Avenue, Toronto, Ontario, Canada M4V 3B2
(a division of Pearson Penguin Canada Inc.)
Penguin Ireland, 25 St Stephen's Green, Dublin 2, Ireland
(a division of Penguin Books Ltd)
Penguin Group (Australia), 250 Camberwell Road, Camberwell, Victoria 3124,
Australia (a division of Pearson Australia Group Pty Ltd)
Penguin Books India Pvt Ltd, 11 Community Centre, Panchsheel Park,
New Delhi – 110 017, India
Penguin Group (NZ), cnr Airborne and Rosedale Roads, Albany, Auckland 1310,
New Zealand (a division of Pearson New Zealand Ltd)
Penguin Books (South Africa) (Pty) Ltd, 24 Sturdee Avenue, Rosebank,
Johannesburg 2196, South Africa

Penguin Books Ltd, Registered Offices: 80 Strand, London WC2R 0RL, England

www.penguin.com

First published 2005
1

Made and printed in England by Clays Ltd, St Ives plc

British Library Cataloguing in Publication Data
A CIP catalogue record for this book is available from the British Library
ISBN-13: 978–0–141–31929–1

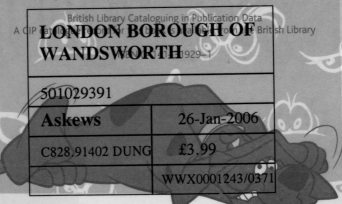

SCOOBY-DOO!™
Terror-rific Joke Book

Richard Dungworth

PUFFIN

What do you get if you let Shaggy roam about as he pleases?

A free-range chicken.

How does the 10,000 Volt Ghost feel first thing in the morning?

Shocking.

Why is Fred a rubbish boyfriend?

He's always wanting to split up.

SHAGGY: Hey, Scoob – how does the Beast of Bottomless Lake like his pizza?

SCOOBY: Ry ron't ro, Raggy . . .

SHAGGY: Like, **deep pan**, old buddy!

Which Mystery Inc.
member is hopeless with
dried plums?
Disaster-prune Daphne.

Which spook has four legs,
long hair and fangs?
Yakula.

What does Velma use to
write up her case notes?
Mystery Ink.

What does Shaggy like on his apple pie?

Cowardy custard.

What does Redbeard's Ghost watch in the evening?

Pirate videos.

What's the difference between a Mystery Inc. adventure and a crazy astronaut?

One's a spooky case, man, and the other's a kooky spaceman.

SHAGGY: Zoinks! Like, what's that vampire doing dancing?

VELMA: I think it's the Fangdango . . .

Does the ghostly
Miner 49er keep his
home tidy?

No, it's a pit.

What do you need to hand-sew
your own ghost trap?

A needle and Fred.

SHAGGY: Like, what do you get if you steal a baby ghost's rattle, Scoob?

SCOOBY: Ri ron't ro, Raggy . . .

SHAGGY: A phantom tantrum!

Why shouldn't you tease the Wax Phantom?

In case he has a meltdown.

SHAGGY: Hey, Scoob, like which *real* scary Scottish beast always rings your doorbell?

SCOOBY: Ri ron't ro, Raggy. Rich ron?

SHAGGY: The Knock Less monster!

What part of mystery-solving are dogs really good at?

Following leads.

What have Hans Christian Andersen and Scooby got in common?

They're both Great Danes.

What does the Snow Ghost like to do at the weekend?

Chill out and take things freezy.

What happens if you bump
into the Tar Monster?

You come to a sticky end.

What do you call
a gang of ghost-
detecting pigs?

Mystery Oink.

What's yellow and
can see just as well
in all directions?

**Shaggy with his
eyes tight shut.**

What's found in haunted houses and smells nasty?

Scooby-Doo-doo.

What's the difference between Shaggy and the 10:15 train to Coolsville?

The 10:15 doesn't always run.

What do you call a Great Dane blowing into a musical instrument?

Scooby-Didgeridoo.

What should
you feed a
crazy
Apeman?

Monkey nuts.

VELMA: Hey, Shaggy – do you
remember when Fred came up
with that 'jelly and
blancmange' ghost trap?

SHAGGY: Was that the one that took,
like, forever to set?

Why does the Black Knight sleep during the day?

He works the knight shift.

What do you say to a daft dog holding a wax doll with pins in?

'Do you do Voodoo, Scooby-Doo?'

What's hairy, found in spooky places and will eat anything?

Shaggy.

DAPHNE: Jeepers! That caveman we defrosted sure has got the giggles . . .

VELMA: Uh-huh. I think he's an example of Prehysteric Man . . .

What happens every time Velma drops her glasses?

She makes a spectacle of herself.

Where can you learn more about the Spooky Space Kook?

In a kookery book.

What do you get if you freeze-dry Scrappy-Doo?

Puppy powder.

What do you call a gang of super-sleuths who've just eaten Aubergine-and-Egg-Chilli-à-la-Shaggy?

Mystery Stink.

HOT

SHAGGY: Zoinks! Like, where did that vampire go?

VELMA: I think he just popped out for a bite.

What do you call a daft dog wearing flippers and an air-tank?

A Scooby diver.

Why is it pointless asking Skeleton Men for a helping hand?

They're bone idle.

What's the difference between a worn-out jumper and Mystery Inc.'s leader with no clothes on?

One's threadbare and the other's bare Fred.

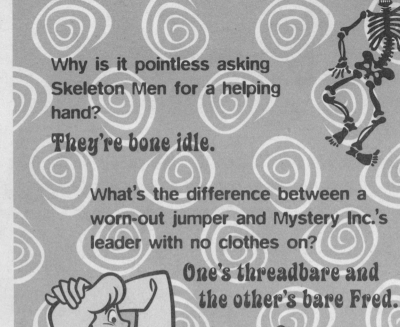

When do Daphne's pink tights help with an escape?

When they have a ladder in them.

FRED: Look, Velma – a long stick with a chalked tip, covered in glowing fingerprints . . .

VELMA: Jinkies! It's a snooker clue!

Why didn't Scooby
bite the Ghost Clown?
In case he tasted funny.

What do you call someone who's
obsessed with the Mystery Machine?
A vanatic.

Why did the coffin cry?

He'd lost his mummy.

What do you get if
you cross Velma with
a pair of wooden shoes?

Clever clogs.

Which trousers did Shaggy use
to signal for help?

His distressed flares.

RIP

Why did the 10,000 Volt Ghost complain to the waiter?

He'd been overcharged.

FRED: Why's Scooby making that ticking noise?

SHAGGY: Like, he's training to be a watchdog, man.

What happened
when Shaggy fell
in a vat of starch?

**He was scared
stiff.**

What should you
do if you meet
the Gator Ghoul?

**Run – and
make it
snappy.**

Does Scooby wear a sunhat
when it's hot?

No, just pants.

What do you call an Apeman with a banana in each ear?

Anything you like, he can't hear you.

What's purple and spends a lot of time gagged and tied to a chair?

A damson in distress.

What do you call a chicken that can't lay eggs?

Shaggy.

What instrument do Skeleton Men play?

The trom-bone.

What do you say to an irritating puppy who's threatening to leave your gang?

'Scrappy, do.'

What should you do if you
catch a *real* monster?

Keep your trap shut.

I have scaly skin, red eyes
and fangs – what am I?

Ugly.

FRED: Strange – I can't seem to get the Mystery Machine to move.

DAPHNE: Perhaps you're in the wrong gear?

FRED: Nah – blue slacks and shirt, white pullover, stylish necktie – this is what I always wear . . .

What has sixteen wheels but no tail lights?

Scooby on roller skates.

What did Fred say when he caught
the mummy by its bandages?

'Let's wrap it up.'

Which ghost is
very messy with
his tomato
soup?

Redbeard.

What do
you call a
thirty-layer
multi-decker
Shaggy
sandwich?

Half made.

Which ghost has no
head but a sore
throat?

**The Headless
Hoarse Man.**

Which part of being
ghost-napped does
Daphne find most
amusing?

The gags.

What do you call
a booby-trap that
doesn't work?

A rubbish chute.

Which zombies always
get girlfriends?

The good-lurking ones.

What does Velma use
to see creepy villains
more clearly?

Spook-tacles.

What does Shaggy's dog
sleep under?

A Scooby-Doo-vet.

Which side of the Wolfman should
you try to stay on?

The outside.

SHAGGY: Make like an insect, old pal!

SCOOBY: Ruh?

SHAGGY: Like, *flee*!

What's the difference between Scooby Doo and Shaggy's chin?

Scooby's had LOTS of close shaves.

What's Dr Jekyll's favourite party game?

Hyde-and-sneak.

SHAGGY: Hey, Scoob, old pal – like, what sounds cold, but feels hot?

SCOOBY: Ri ron't ro. Rot rounds rold, rut reels rot?

SHAGGY: Like, *chilli* sauce, man!

Is a gold-digger's ghost a big deal for Mystery Inc.?

No, just a miner problem.

What happened to Fred's high-school rock band?

They split up.

What do you get if you cross a Great Dane with a rooster?

Scooby-cock-a-doodle-Doo.

How did Shaggy and Scoob first spot the Demon Shark?

They saw some fin moving.

What do you call a vehicle full of Daphne's clothes?

A purple carrier.

What do you get if
you put Shaggy's best
friend in the freezer?
Ice Scoobs.

How does the
Beast of Bottomless
Lake cook chips?
In a deep fryer.

When is a tap like Shaggy?
When it's running.

How does Charlie, the out-of-control robot, keep in shape?
Circuit training.

What do you get if you cross Scrappy-Doo with a cat?
Puppy purr.

Why are the quiet Owl Men the ones to fear most?

Because they just don't give a hoot.

FRED: We're trying to track down Dr Jekyll and the Wolfman . . .

LOCAL: Sorry, I haven't seen Hyde nor hair of them.

What do you get if you give Shaggy's dog a notepad and pencil?

Scooby-Doodles.

Which ghoul has a bolt through his neck and food all down his front?

Frankenstain.

When is a Mystery Inc. mystery like an egg?

When they crack it.

What kind of dried fruit does
the 10,000 Volt Ghost like best?
Currants.

What do you call
a daft dog with udders?
Scooby-Moo.

SHAGGY: Hey, Scoob, if you hold a werewolf's nose, how does he smell?

SCOOBY: Ri ron't ro, Raggy, row?

SHAGGY: Like, pretty dreadful, old buddy!

What do you call a pot of melted Scooby Snax?

Scooby-Fon-Doo.

What did the Miner 49er say when Scooby got away?

'Dog-gone!'

When is a rooster like Shaggy?

When it acts like a chicken.

What's the only kind of witch that Shaggy likes?

A multi-decker submarine sand-witch.

What line of work is the Apeman in?

Monkey business.

When is Shaggy at his most charming?

When he's dashing.

Where do haunted suits of armour study?

Knight school.

What do you get if you cover Scooby in icing sugar and currants?

A Great Danish pastry.

What kind of fuel does the Momba Zombie's car use?

Undeaded.

SHAGGY: Like, there you go – one monster-sized quiche, just like Fred said.

VELMA: Hmmm . . . are you sure he said 'What we need is a flan' . . .?

What sort of booby-trap does Daphne prefer?

A fashion chute.

Where did Scooby go when his tail fell off?

A high street re-tailer.

How come the Wax Phantom is so hard to spot?

He just melts into the background.

What's Shaggy's favourite fast food?

Terri-fried chicken.

SHAGGY: Hey, Scoob, old pal –
do you know why I can't
stand vampires?

SCOOBY: Ry, Raggy?

SHAGGY: Like, because they're a real
pain in the neck, man!

What do you call Scooby's
nephew in a bad mood?

Snappy-Doo.

How do you get ten zombies in the Mystery Machine?

Three and a half in the front, six and a half in the back.

When does the Technicolour Phantom feel fed up?

When he's blue.

Who is Shaggy's favourite band?

The Red Hot Chilli Peppers.

HOT

What do Mystery Inc. groupies
send the Mystery Machine?

Van mail.

Which spook never wears
a cycle helmet?

The Headless Spectre.

What do you call it when Shaggy falls out with his dog?

A Scooby-to-Doo.

What do Scooby and Shaggy do in a pet-food shop?

Split up and search for chews.

Whose catchphrase is: 'Puppy power, or whatever'?
Slaphappy-Doo.

Is the 10,000 Volt Ghost a good public speaker?
Yes, he's electrifying.

What's Velma's favourite kind of music?
Case notes.

What can you use to stick down
Shaggy's dog?

Scooby-Glue.

What do you get if you
cross the Snow Ghost
with a porcupine?

A real spine-chiller.

What did Shaggy say when the Beast of Bottomless Lake cornered him and Scooby?

'Like, we're in deep water now, Scoob!'

What's the difference between a coyote, and the Wolfman's fleas?

One howls on the prairie, the other prowls on the hairy.

What's the difference between an oiled cow's foot and Shaggy?

One's a slippy hoof, the other's a hippy sleuth.

Who's the best Mystery Inc. member to invite to a posh do?

Velma, because she's the smartest.

SHAGGY: Hey, Scoob, what do spooks like on their sausage and mash?

SCOOBY: Rih ron't ro . . .

SHAGGY: Like, *grave*-y, old pal!

What do you call a gang of really grumpy ghost detectives?

Misery Inc.

What the difference between a tropical fruit seller and Scooby?

One's got pawpaws, and the other's got four paws.

What's the best way to find a zombie?

Visit a graveyard and see what you can dig up.

SHAGGY: Hey, Scooby, when spooks play soccer, who wears the number one shirt?

SCOOBY: Roo, Raggy?

SHAGGY: Like, the ghoul-keeper, old buddy!

When the Momba Zombie races the Snow Ghost, who wins?

Nobody – it's a dead heat.

SHAGGY: Hey, Velma, like what's yellow and runs off?

VELMA: Errmm . . . that's you, isn't it, Shaggy?

SHAGGY: Nope – a banana split!

How does Redbeard's Ghost check his shelves are straight?

With a spirit level.

When is Fred like a golf club?

When he's the driver.

What do you call a
female phantom?

Mona.

DAPHNE: Jeeepers, Freddy!
The road is completely
blocked by zombies!

FRED: Yup, I guess it's a
dead end . . .

What sort of jokes does
Scooby tell best?
Shaggy-dog stories.

Are zombies good at rollerblading?
No, they're rotten.

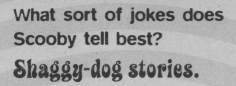

What do Tar Monsters
do in a crisis?
Stick together.

What's Shaggy's
favourite country?
Chile.

HOT

What do you call
a Great Dane who's
completely lost the plot?
Scooby-Doolally.

What's Shaggy's favourite
burger chain?
Wimpy.

Why shouldn't you put Shaggy and
Scooby in your washing?
They're guaranteed to run.

What goes: 'Relp! BOING! BOING!'
Scooby-Roo.